Introduction

This book supports students preparing for the SQA Natic
papers in the book are carefully modelled after past papei
board to ensure that the papers as a whole provide a rich and varied practice to meet all
requirements of SQA National 5 Maths with an appropriate difficulty.

Papers are designed to teach students the most easily applicable, reusable and fastest
solutions to typical problems, and utilise problems which target areas of maths which
students typically forget under the pressure of an exam. Solutions provided have been
reviewed by many students to ensure that they are easily understandable while being the
fastest and most re-applicable.

Each practice paper covers the following six distinct topic areas:
1. Fundamental Numerical Operations
2. Algebra
3. Geometry
4. Trigonometry
5. Statistics
6. Reasoning

After completing these practice papers, you should be able to:
1. Quickly formulate optimal solutions to any SQA National 5 maths question
2. More readily apply previously learnt skills on a question to question basis

SQA National 5 Maths Practice Papers comprises of 2 books, calculator and non-calculator.
Each book contains 4 full practice papers. For the book with calculator, each practice paper
contains 18 questions and solutions. The non-calculator book contains 15 questions and
solutions per paper.

Contents

Paper 1   Calculator

Materials

For this paper you must have:
- a calculator
- mathematical instruments

Time allowed

1 hour 50 minutes.

Instructions

- Use blue or black ink pen. Draw diagrams in pencil.
- Answer all questions.
- You must answer the questions in the space provided. Do not write outside the box around each page or on blank pages.
- Do all rough work in this book. Cross through any work that you do not want to be marked.
- State the units for your answer where appropriate.
- In all calculations, show clearly how you work out your answer.

Information

- The marks for questions are shown in brackets.
- The maximum mark for this paper is 60.

1   A clothes shop has a sale.

In the sale, normal prices are reduced by 15%.

1(a)   The normal price of a T-shirt is £12.

Calculate the sale price of the T-shirt.

....

....

....

Answer…………………………….   (2 marks)

1(b)   The price of a jacket is reduced by £6.00 in the sale.

Calculate the normal price of the jacket.

....

....

....

Answer…………………………….   (2 marks)

2   The speed of light is approximately 3×10^5 km/s. What distance would the light have travelled after one minute?

Give your answer in scientific notation.

....

....

....

Answer…………………………….   (2 marks)

3   80% of p=20% of q.

Work out p as a percentage of q.

....

....

....

Answer…………………………….   (2 marks)

4   Solve $x^2 - 3x - 9 = 0$

Give your answers to 2 decimal places.

....

....

....

Answer............................   (2 marks)

5   Solve the equation $4\cos x° + 2 = 3$, $0 \le x < 360$.

Give your answers to 1 decimal place.

....

....

....

Answer............................   (2 marks)

6   State the maximum and minimum values of $y = 3\sin x°$ and its period.

....

....

....

Answer............................   (3 marks)

7   Express $x^2 + 8x - 15$ in the form $(x + p)^2 + q$.

....

....

....

Answer............................   (2 marks)

8   Expand and simplify $(4x - 3y)(3x + 4y)$

....

....

....

Answer............................   (2 marks)

9   Simplify $\dfrac{a^4 \times 3a}{a^{-2}}$.

....

....

....

Answer…………………………….   (2 marks)

10   Factorise fully $(a-b)^2 + (a-b)(a+3b)$.

....

....

....

Answer…………………………….   (2 marks)

11   ABCD is a kite.

Diagram **NOT** accurately drawn

AB = 5 cm, BC = 10 cm, $\angle BAD = 110°$

Calculate the area of kite ABCD.

Give your answer to 3 significant figures.

....

....

....

....

....

....

....

....

Answer…………………………….   (4 marks)

12   A hollow right circular cone, **A**, has height 20 cm and radius 5 cm.

The cone is held with its axis vertical and its vertex at the bottom.

A funnel is formed by removing the right circular cone, **B**, of height 8 cm from the

bottom of **A**, as shown on the diagram.

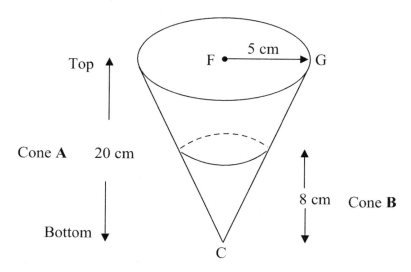

12(a)   Calculate the radius, in cm, of cone **B**.

....

....

....

        Answer................................   (3 marks)

12(b)   Calculate the volume, in cm³, of the funnel.

Give your answer in terms of π.

....

....

....

....

....

....

        Answer................................   (3 marks)

13   When I am at point A, the angle of elevation of the top of a tree T is 30°, but if I

walk 20 m towards the tree, to point B, the angle of elevation is then 50°.

13(a)   Work out the distance TB.

Give your answer to 1 decimal place.

....

....

....

....

....

....

    Answer................................   (3 marks)

13(b)   Work out the height of the tree.

Give your answer to 1 decimal place.

....

....

....

    Answer................................   (3 marks)

14   The pendulum of a clock swings along an arc of a circle, centre O.

The pendulum swings through an angle of $65°$, travelling from A to B. The length of the pendulum is 25 cm.

Take $\pi = 3.14$.

Calculate the length of arc AB.

Give your answer to 2 decimal places.

....

....

....

....

....

....

           Answer.................................   (3 marks)

15   The outer square has area k cm², points A, B, C and D are quarter of the ways along the sides, as shown.

Work out the area of square ABCD in terms of k.

....

....

....

....

....

....

           Answer.................................   (4 marks)

16   ABC and DEA are straight lines. BE is parallel to CD. $\angle$DAC $= 45°$, $\angle$ACD $= 50°$

Work out the size of $\angle$AEB .

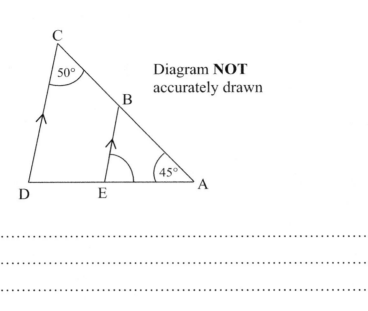

Diagram **NOT**
accurately drawn

....

....

....

....

....

....

Answer…………………………….   (4 marks)

4

17   ABCDEFGH is a cuboid.

AB = 20 units, BC = 10 units, BF = 12 units

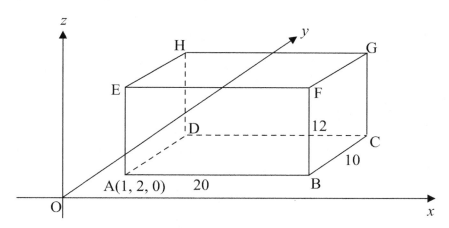

Edges AB, DC, EF and HG are parallel to the *x*-axis. Edges BC, AD, EH and FG are parallel to the *y*-axis. The base ABCD is on the ground.

The coordinates of A are (1, 2, 0).

17(a)   Write down the coordinates of G.

....

....

....

....

....

Answer............................   (3 marks)

17(b)   Calculate $\left|\overrightarrow{AG}\right|$, the magnitude of $\overrightarrow{AG}$.

Give your answer to 1 decimal place.

....

....

....

Answer............................   (3 marks)

18   OAB is a triangle such that $\overrightarrow{OA} = 2\mathbf{a}$ and $\overrightarrow{AB} = \mathbf{b}$. Point D is the midpoint of OA and

ABC is a straight line such that AB:AC = 4:5.

Express $\overrightarrow{DC}$ in terms of **a** and **b**.

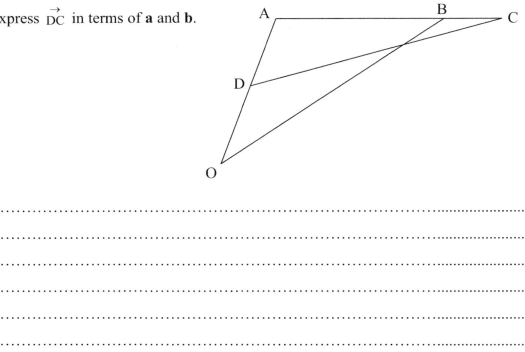

....

....

....

....

....

....

Answer................................   (4 marks)

Paper 2   Calculator

Materials

For this paper you must have:
- a calculator
- mathematical instruments

Time allowed

1 hour 50 minutes.

Instructions

- Use blue or black ink pen. Draw diagrams in pencil.
- Answer all questions.
- You must answer the questions in the space provided. Do not write outside the box around each page or on blank pages.
- Do all rough work in this book. Cross through any work that you do not want to be marked.
- State the units for your answer where appropriate.
- In all calculations, show clearly how you work out your answer.

Information

- The marks for questions are shown in brackets.
- The maximum mark for this paper is 60.

1   Naomi invests £6000 for 5 years. The investment gets compound interest of 5% per annum.

Work out how much the investment is worth at the end of 5 years.

……………………………………………………………………………………………

……………………………………………………………………………………………

……………………………………………………………………………………………

Answer……………………………….   (2 marks)

2   Here are three numbers written in scientific notation.

Arrange these numbers in ascending order.

3.4×10^{-7} 5.5×10^{-8} 2.1×10^{-6}

……………………………………………………………………………………………

……………………………………………………………………………………………

……………………………………………………………………………………………

Answer……………………………….   (2 marks)

3    $x : y = 4 : 5$ and $a : b = 5x : 3y$

Work out $a : b$

Give your answer in its simplest form.

……………………………………………………………………………………………

……………………………………………………………………………………………

……………………………………………………………………………………………

Answer……………………………….   (2 marks)

4   Solve $\dfrac{x}{3} + \dfrac{x+2}{5} = 3$

……………………………………………………………………………………………

……………………………………………………………………………………………

……………………………………………………………………………………………

Answer……………………………….   (2 marks)

8

5   Solve the equation $\tan x° + 3 = 2$, for $0 \le x < 360$.

....

....

....

       Answer................................   (2 marks)

6   State the maximum and minimum values of $y = 5\cos\frac{1}{2}x°$ and its period.

....

....

....

       Answer................................   (3 marks)

7   Express $\dfrac{6}{\sqrt{18}}$ as a fraction with a rational denominator.

    Give your answer in its simplest form.

....

....

....

       Answer................................   (2 marks)

8   Expand and simplify $(\sin x° - \cos x°)^2$.

    Show your working.

....

....

....

       Answer................................   (2 marks)

9

9   Simplify $\dfrac{5a}{2a-1} \times \dfrac{10a-5}{4a^3} \div \dfrac{15}{2a^4}$

....

....

....

     Answer...................................   (2 marks)

10   Factorise fully $3x^3 - 12x$

....

....

....

     Answer...................................   (2 marks)

11   The perimeter of an isosceles triangle flower bed, ABC, is 28 m of rope, with
     $AB = AC$, and $\angle A = 120°$.

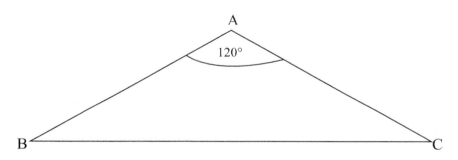

     Work out the length of AB.

     Give your answer to 1 decimal place.

....

....

....

....

....

....

     Answer...................................   (4 marks)

12   A sphere and a cone have the same volume. The base of the cone and the sphere

have the same radius r cm .

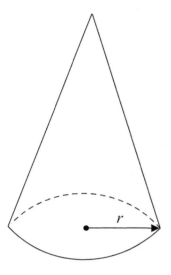 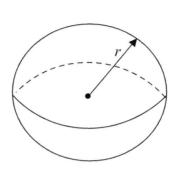

Work out the curved surface area of cone in terms of r.

....

....

....

....

....

....

....

....

....

Answer................................   (4 marks)

4

13   ABC and DEA are straight lines. BE is parallel to CD. ∠AEB = 85°, BE = 8 cm, CD = 10 cm, AE = 6 cm.

Work out the length of AC.

Give your answer to 2 decimal places.

Diagram **NOT** accurately drawn

....

....

....

....

....

....

....

....

....

....

....

....

....

....

Answer................................   (4 marks)

14   This shape consists of a sector of a circle with 2 identical right-angled triangles.

Take $\pi = 3.14$.

Calculate the area of this shape.

Give your answer to 2 decimal places.

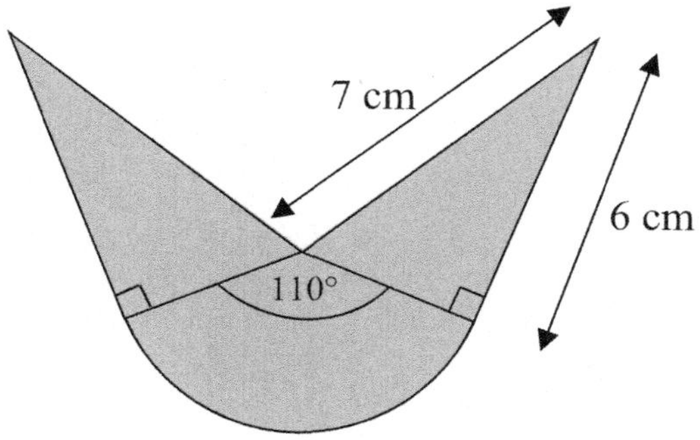

7 cm

6 cm

110°

....

....

....

....

....

....

Answer............................   (5 marks)

15   The diagram shows two circles. One has centre A and a radius of 8 cm. The other

has centre B and a radius of 10 cm. AB = 12 cm and the circles intersect at P and Q.

Calculate the length of PQ.

Give your answer to 1 decimal place.

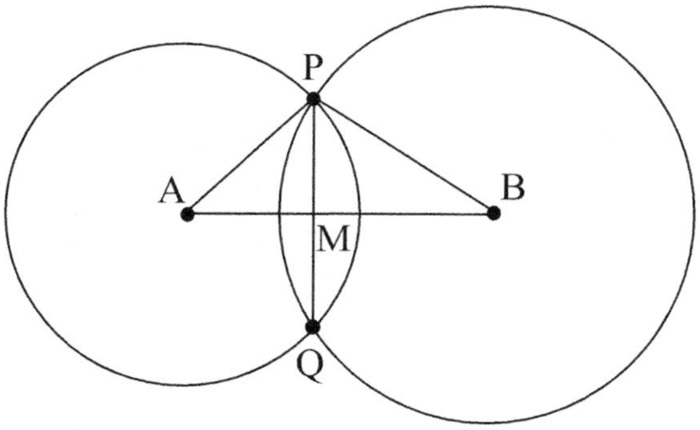

P

A   B

M

Q

....

....

....

....

....

....

Answer............................   (5 marks)

10

17

16   Here is an L-shape. All lengths are in centimetres.

The shape has area A cm^2.

Show that $A = w^2 + x^2 - wx$

....

....

....

....

....

....

....

....

....

(4 marks)

4

17 The tent shown in the diagram has a base that is 2.5 units wide and 4.0 units long. The height of the tent is 1.5 units. The ends are isosceles triangles AE = ED, BF = FC, and perpendicular to the base.

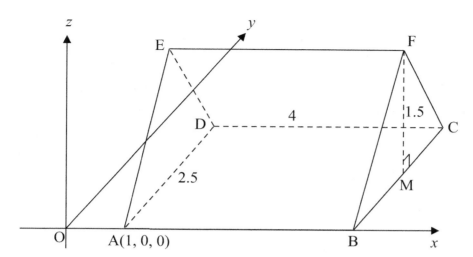

The base ABCD is on the ground. The coordinates of A are (1, 0, 0).

17(a) Find out the coordinates of B.

....

....

....

Answer.................................... (3 marks)

17(b) Find out the coordinates of F.

....

....

....

Answer.................................... (3 marks)

17(c) Calculate $\left|\overrightarrow{BF}\right|$, the magnitude of $\overrightarrow{BF}$.

Give your answer to 2 decimal places.

....

....

....

Answer.................................... (3 marks)

9

19

18   OABC is a parallelogram. BCD is a straight line. BD = 3BC. M is the midpoint of OC.

$\overrightarrow{OA} = \mathbf{x}$, $\overrightarrow{AB} = \mathbf{y}$.

Show by a vector method that AM is parallel to OD.

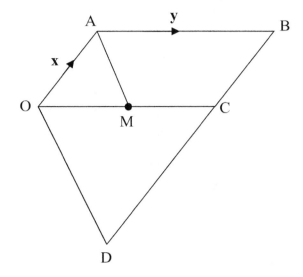

....

....

....

....

....

....

....

....

....

(4 marks)

Paper 3   Calculator

Materials
For this paper you must have:
- a calculator
- mathematical instruments

Time allowed
1 hour 50 minutes.

Instructions
- Use blue or black ink pen. Draw diagrams in pencil.
- Answer all questions.
- You must answer the questions in the space provided. Do not write outside the box around each page or on blank pages.
- Do all rough work in this book. Cross through any work that you do not want to be marked.
- State the units for your answer where appropriate.
- In all calculations, show clearly how you work out your answer.

Information
- The marks for questions are shown in brackets.
- The maximum mark for this paper is 60.

1   Emma buys a jumper.

20% VAT is added to the price of the jumper.

Emma has to pay a total of £60.

What is the price of the jumper with **no** VAT added?

....

....

....

Answer...................................   (2 marks)

2   Work out the value of $2.2 \times 10^5 \times (4 \times 10^3)$

Give your answer in scientific notation.

....

....

....

Answer...................................   (2 marks)

3   Find $|\mathbf{p}|$, the magnitude of vector $\mathbf{p} = \begin{pmatrix} 10 \\ 8 \\ -40 \end{pmatrix}$.

....

....

....

Answer...................................   (2 marks)

4   Solve the simultaneous equations

$2x - 4y = 10$

$2x + y = 30$

....

....

....

....

Answer...................................   (2 marks)

5   Solve the equation $4\sin x° + 3 = 2$, for $0 \le x < 360$.

Give your answers to 1 decimal place.

....

....

....

Answer................................... (2 marks)

6   State the maximum and minimum values of $y = 5\sin 2x° - 2$ and its period.

....

....

....

Answer................................... (3 marks)

7   Express $\dfrac{\sqrt{30}}{\sqrt{2}}$ as a fraction with a rational denominator.

Give your answer in its simplest form.

....

....

....

Answer................................... (2 marks)

8   Expand and simplify $(\sqrt{x} + \dfrac{1}{\sqrt{x}})^2$, where $x > 0$.

Show your working.

....

....

....

Answer................................... (2 marks)

9

9   Simplify $\dfrac{x^2 - 2x + 1}{x^2 - 6x + 5}$, $x \neq 1$, $x \neq 5$

....

....

....

Answer................................   (2 marks)

10   Factorise fully $4c^3d - 9cd^3$

....

....

....

Answer................................   (2 marks)

11   Here is a triangle.

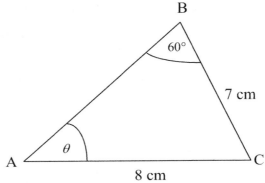

Work out the angle θ .

Give your answer to 1 decimal place.

....

....

....

....

....

....

Answer................................   (5 marks)

12   The diagram shows a solid prism. The top EFGH is a rectangle of width 20 cm and length 30 cm, the base ABCD is rectangle of width 20 cm and length 50 cm. The line joining the centres of the top and the base is perpendicular to both and is 40 cm long.

Work out the volume of the prism.

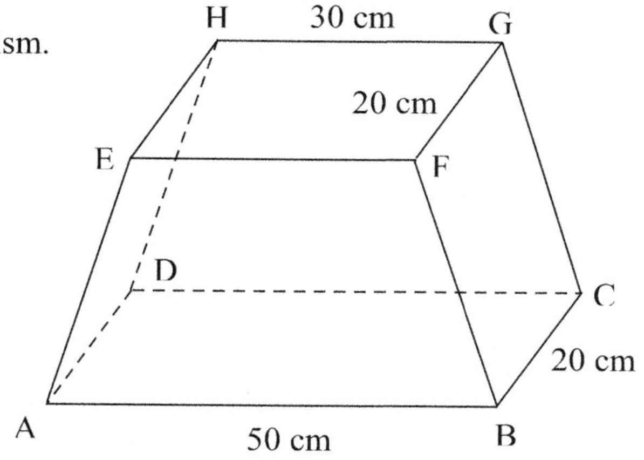

Answer……………………………….   (5 marks)

13   The diagram shows triangle ABC. AB = AC.

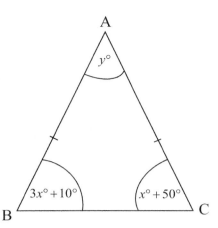

Find the value of $y°$.

Show your working clearly.

....

....

....

....

....

    Answer............................   (5 marks)

14   The shape consists of two overlapping circles below.

Find the perimeter of this shape.

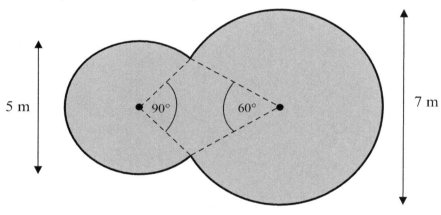

Take $\pi = 3.14$.

Give your answer to 2 decimal places.

....

....

....

....

    Answer............................   (5 marks)

10

15   A hot air balloon is hovering above the ground. Emma and Jack are looking up at
the hot air balloon. In the diagram below, E, J and B represent the positions of
Emma, Jack and the balloon respectively.

The angle of elevation of the balloon from Emma is 55° .

The angle of elevation of the balloon from Jack is 36° .

Emma and Jack are 450 metres apart on level ground.

Calculate the height of the hot air balloon above the ground.

Give your answer to 1 decimal place.

....

....

....

....

....

....

         Answer...............................   (5 marks)

16   A company produces mugs in two sizes.

Small mugs are 6 cm high and can hold 100 cm^3 of liquid.

Large mugs are 12 cm high and are identical in shape to small mugs.

Work out the volume of a large mug.

....

....

....

....

....

....

         Answer...............................   (4 marks)

5

17 ABCD is a pyramid. *A*BC is an isosceles triangle with AB = AC = 10 units and BC = 12 units. BCD is an isosceles triangle with BD = CD = 26 units. D is vertically above A and $\angle BAD = \angle CAD = 90°$.

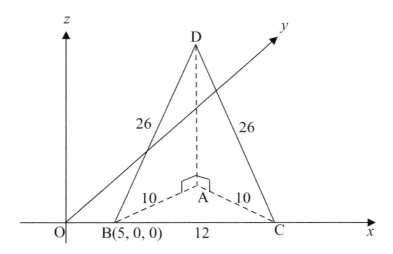

The base ABC is on the ground. The coordinates of B are (5, 0, 0).

Find out the coordinates of D.

....

....

....

....

....

....

....

....

....

Answer................................   (5 marks)

18   PQR is a triangle. W is the midpoint of PQ. X is the point on QR such that

$QX:XR = 3:1$. PRY is a straight line. $\overrightarrow{PQ} = \mathbf{a}$, $\overrightarrow{PR} = \mathbf{b}$, $PR:RY = 2:1$.

Use a vector method to show that WXY is a straight line.

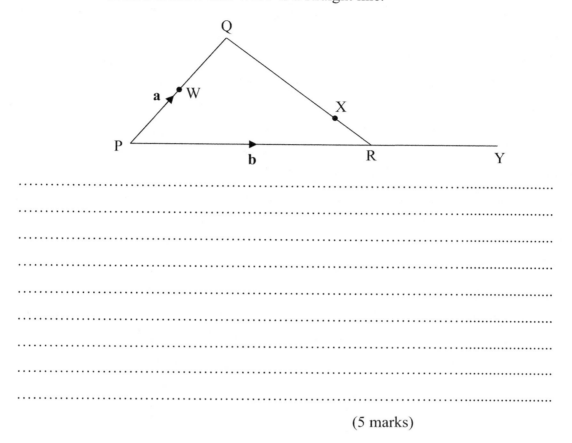

....

....

....

....

....

....

....

....

....

(5 marks)

Paper 4   Calculator

Materials

For this paper you must have:

- a calculator
- mathematical instruments

Time allowed

1 hour 50 minutes.

Instructions

- Use blue or black ink pen. Draw diagrams in pencil.
- Answer all questions.
- You must answer the questions in the space provided. Do not write outside the box around each page or on blank pages.
- Do all rough work in this book. Cross through any work that you do not want to be marked.
- State the units for your answer where appropriate.
- In all calculations, show clearly how you work out your answer.

Information

- The marks for questions are shown in brackets.
- The maximum mark for this paper is 60.

1   An antiques dealer buys a vase for £400. He sells the vase for 50% more than the price he paid for it.

For how much does the dealer sell the vase?

....

....

....

Answer................................   (2 marks)

2   A sunflower seed weighs 3.5×10^{-5} kilograms, the weight of a sesame seed is 9% of the weight of a sunflower seed.

Calculate the weight of a sesame seed in kilograms.

Give your answer in scientific notation.

....

....

....

Answer................................   (2 marks)

3   Calculate the distance from A(10, 15, 32) to B(6, 9, 20).

....

....

....

Answer................................   (2 marks)

4   Emma is solving $3x^2 + 9x = 0$

She uses the following method:

$3x^2 + 9x = 0$ $\xrightarrow{\text{subtract } 9x \text{ from both sides}}$ $3x^2 = -9x$ $\xrightarrow{\text{divide both sides by } 3x}$ $x = -3$

Evaluate her method and her answer.

....

....

....

Answer................................   (2 marks)

8

5   Solve $25\sin^2 x° = 1$ for $0 \leq x < 360$.

Give your answers to 1 decimal place.

....

....

....

....

....

Answer............................   (4 marks)

6   State the maximum and minimum values of $y = 5\sin(x - 50)° + 3$ and its period.

....

....

....

Answer............................   (3 marks)

7   Express $\sqrt{2} + \dfrac{8}{\sqrt{2}}$ as a fraction with a rational denominator.

Give your answer in its simplest form.

....

....

....

Answer............................   (2 marks)

8   Write as a single fraction $\dfrac{10}{x^2 - 25} - \dfrac{1}{x - 5}$, $x \neq 5$, $x \neq -5$

Give your answer in its simplest form.

....

....

....

Answer............................   (2 marks)

11

9 Simplify $(2x^3y^2)^4$

....

....

....

Answer................................... (2 marks)

10 Factorise fully $(x+5)^3 - (x+5)^2(x-5)$.

....

....

....

Answer................................... (2 marks)

11 Triangle ABC has perimeter 16cm

AB = 5 cm.

BC = 4 cm.

Calculate the size of the biggest angle in triangle ABC.

Give your answer to 1 decimal place.

....

....

....

....

....

....

Answer................................... (3 marks)

12   Solid **A** and Solid **B** are mathematically similar.

Solid **A** has a volume of 50 cm³

Solid **A** has surface area 30 cm²

Solid **B** has surface area 270 cm²

Calculate the volume of solid **B**.

………………………………………………………………………………………………

………………………………………………………………………………………………

………………………………………………………………………………………………

………………………………………………………………………………………………

………………………………………………………………………………………………

Answer……………………………….   (3 marks)

13   PQRS is an isosceles trapezium. Each side of the trapezium is a tangent to the circle.

The radius of the circle is r cm.

13(a)   Work out the perimeter of the isosceles trapezium.

Give your answer in terms of r.

………………………………………………………………………………………………

………………………………………………………………………………………………

………………………………………………………………………………………………

………………………………………………………………………………………………

………………………………………………………………………………………………

………………………………………………………………………………………………

Answer……………………………….   (3 marks)

13(b) Work out the area of the shaded region.

Give your answer in terms of r.

....

....

....

....

Answer................................   (3 marks)

14   The base for a rocking horse is made from the arc of a circular piece of wood, with a triangular section ABO cut off. The radius of the circle is 90 cm and $\angle AOB = 62°$. Take $\pi = 3.14$.

Give your answer to 2 decimal places.

O

62°

90 cm   90 cm

16 cm

Base

A   B

14(a) Calculate the area of the segment.

....

....

....

Answer................................   (3 marks)

14(b) Calculate the volume of wood used to make the base (16 cm wide) of the rocking horse.

....

....

....

Answer................................   (3 marks)

9

15   Three lighthouses, A, B and C are situated on the seaside.

Lighthouse A is 30 km due south of lighthouse B.

Lighthouse B is 50 km from lighthouse C.

Lighthouse C is on a bearing of 120° from lighthouse A.

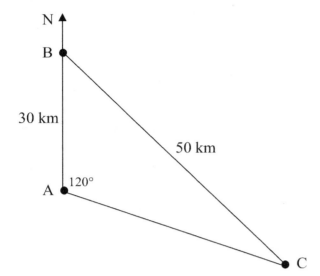

Calculate the bearing of lighthouse C from lighthouse B.

....

....

....

Answer............................   (3 marks)

16   $A(1\frac{1}{2}, \frac{1}{4})$, $B(2\frac{1}{2}, 2\frac{1}{4})$ and $C(3, 3\frac{1}{4})$ are points on a coordinate grid. Show that

the three points are on a straight line.

....

....

....

....

....

....

....

....

(4 marks)

7

17   ABCDEFGH is a basket. The top ABCD is a square of side 35 units and the base
      EFGH is square of side 25 units. The line joining the centres of the top and the base
      is perpendicular to both and is 40 units long.

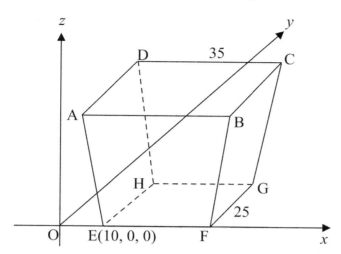

The base EFGH is on the ground. The coordinates of E are (10, 0, 0).

17(a) Find out the coordinates of C.

      ....

      ....

      ....

      ....

      ....

            Answer............................   (3 marks)

17(b) Calculate $\left|\overrightarrow{EC}\right|$, the magnitude of $\overrightarrow{EC}$.

      Give your answer to 1 decimal place.

      ....

      ....

      ....

      ....

      ....

            Answer............................   (3 marks)

6

18   ABCDEFGH is a cuboid.

K lies one quarter of the way along HG.

L lies one third of the way along FG.

$\overrightarrow{AD} = \mathbf{u}$, $\overrightarrow{AB} = \mathbf{v}$, $\overrightarrow{AE} = \mathbf{w}$

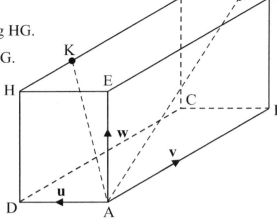

18(a)   Find the vector $\overrightarrow{AK}$, in terms of **u**, **v** and **w**.

....

....

....

....

....

Answer................................   (3 marks)

18(b)   Find the vector $\overrightarrow{AL}$, in terms of **u**, **v** and **w**.

....

....

....

Answer................................   (3 marks)

Paper 1 solutions

1   A clothes shop has a sale.

In the sale, normal prices are reduced by 15%.

1(a)   The normal price of a T-shirt is £12.

Calculate the sale price of the T-shirt.

$12 \times (1 - 15\%) = 10.20$

Answer   £10.20   (2 marks)

1(b)   The price of a jacket is reduced by £6.00 in the sale.

Calculate the normal price of the jacket.

$x \times 15\% = 6 \Rightarrow x = 40$

Answer   £40.00   (2 marks)

2   The speed of light is approximately 3×10^5 km/s. What distance would the light have travelled after one minute?

Give your answer in scientific notation.

$3 \times 10^5 \times 60 = 1.8 \times 10^7$

Answer 1.8×10^7 km   (2 marks)

3   80% of p=20% of q.

Work out p as a percentage of q.

$80\%p = 20\%q \Rightarrow p = \dfrac{1}{4}q \Rightarrow p = 25\%q$

Answer $p = 25\%q$ (2 marks)

4   Solve $x^2 - 3x - 9 = 0$

Give your answers to 2 decimal places.

$x^2 - 3x - 9 = 0 \Rightarrow x = \dfrac{3 \pm \sqrt{9 + 36}}{2} = \dfrac{3 \pm 3\sqrt{5}}{2} \Rightarrow x = 4.85 \ \text{or} \ x = -1.85$

Answer   4.85, -1.85   (2 marks)

10

5   Solve the equation $4\cos x° + 2 = 3$, $0 \leq x < 360$.

Give your answers to 1 decimal place.

$$4\cos x° + 2 = 3 \Rightarrow \cos x° = \frac{1}{4} \Rightarrow x° = 75.5° \text{ or } x° = 360° - 75.5° = 284.5°$$

Answer   75.5°, 284.5°   (2 marks)

6   State the maximum and minimum values of $y = 3\sin x°$ and its period.

$$-1 \leq \sin x° \leq 1 \Rightarrow -3 \leq 3\sin x° \leq 3, \text{ its period: } 360°$$

Answer   minimum: -3, maximum: 3, period: 360°

(3 marks)

7   Express $x^2 + 8x - 15$ in the form $(x + p)^2 + q$.

$$x^2 + 8x - 15 = (x + 4)^2 - 16 - 15 = (x + 4)^2 - 31$$

Answer $(x + 4)^2 - 31$ (2 marks)

8   Expand and simplify $(4x - 3y)(3x + 4y)$

$$(4x - 3y)(3x + 4y) = 12x^2 + 16xy - 9xy - 12y^2 = 12x^2 + 7xy - 12y^2$$

Answer $12x^2 + 7xy - 12y^2$ (2 marks)

9   Simplify $\dfrac{a^4 \times 3a}{a^{-2}}$.

$$\frac{a^4 \times 3a}{a^{-2}} = 3a^{4+1+2} = 3a^7$$

Answer $3a^7$ (2 marks)

10   Factorise fully $(a - b)^2 + (a - b)(a + 3b)$.

$$(a - b)^2 + (a - b)(a + 3b) = (a - b)(a - b + a + 3b) = (a - b)(2a + 2b) = 2(a - b)(a + b)$$

Answer $2(a - b)(a + b)$ (2 marks)

13

11   ABCD is a kite.

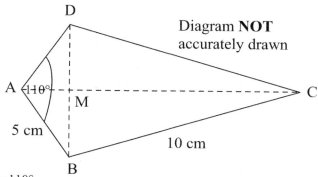

Diagram **NOT** accurately drawn

AB = 5 cm, BC = 10 cm, ∠BAD = 110°

Calculate the area of kite ABCD.

Give your answer to 3 significant figures.

Draw the lines AC and BD. They intersects at M. AC is perpendicular to BD.

In the right-angled triangle AMB, $AM = AB \times \cos \angle MAB = 5 \times \cos \dfrac{110°}{2} = 2.868$,

$BM = AB \times \sin \angle MAB = 5 \times \sin \dfrac{110°}{2} = 4.096$

In the right-angled triangle BMC, $MC = \sqrt{BC^2 - BM^2} = \sqrt{10^2 - 4.096^2} = 9.123$

The area of kite ABCD is

$\dfrac{BD \times AC}{2} = \dfrac{2BM \times (AM + MC)}{2} = BM \times (AM + MC) = 4.096 \times (2.868 + 9.123) = 49.1$

    Answer   49.1 cm²   (4 marks)

12   A hollow right circular cone, **A**, has height 20 cm and radius 5 cm.

The cone is held with its axis vertical and its vertex at the bottom.

A funnel is formed by removing the right circular cone, **B**, of height 8 cm from the

bottom of **A**, as shown on the diagram.

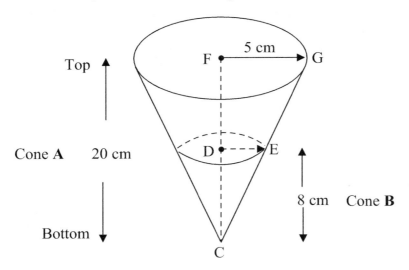

12(a)   Calculate the radius, in cm, of cone **B**.

Triangle CDE is similar to triangle CFG

$$\frac{DE}{FG} = \frac{CD}{CF} \Rightarrow DE = FG \times \frac{CD}{CF} = 5 \times \frac{8}{20} = 2$$

Answer   2 cm   (3 marks)

12(b)   Calculate the volume, in cm³, of the funnel.

Give your answer in terms of π.

The volume of the funnel is

$$\frac{\pi \times FG^2}{3} \times CF - \frac{\pi \times DE^2}{3} \times CD = \frac{\pi \times 5^2}{3} \times 20 - \frac{\pi \times 2^2}{3} \times 8 = 156\pi$$

Answer 156π cm³   (3 marks)

13 When I am at point A, the angle of elevation of the top of a tree T is $30°$, but if I walk 20 m towards the tree, to point B, the angle of elevation is then $50°$.

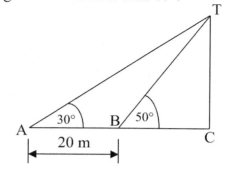

13(a) Work out the distance TB.

Give your answer to 1 decimal place.

$\angle ABT = 180° - \angle CBT = 180° - 50° = 130°$

$\angle ATB = 180° - \angle ABT - \angle A = 180° - 130° - 30° = 20°$

In triangle ABT, $\dfrac{BT}{\sin \angle A} = \dfrac{AB}{\sin \angle ATB} \Rightarrow BT = \dfrac{AB}{\sin \angle ATB} \times \sin \angle A = \dfrac{20}{\sin 20°} \times \sin 30° = 29.2$

Answer   29.2 m   (3 marks)

13(b) Work out the height of the tree.

Give your answer to 1 decimal place.

$CT = BT \times \sin 50° = 29.2 \times \sin 50° = 22.4$

Answer   22.4 m   (3 marks)

14 The pendulum of a clock swings along an arc of a circle, centre O.

The pendulum swings through an angle of $65°$, travelling from A to B. The length of the pendulum is 25 cm.

Take $\pi = 3.14$.

Calculate the length of arc AB.

Give your answer to 2 decimal places.

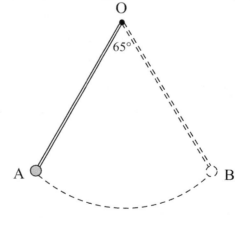

$2\pi r \times \dfrac{65}{360} = 2 \times 3.14 \times 25 \times \dfrac{65}{360} = 28.35$

Answer   28.35 cm   (3 marks)

15   The outer square has area k cm², points A, B, C and D are quarter of the ways along the sides, as shown.

Work out the area of square ABCD in terms of k.

The length of a side of the outer square is a cm.

The length of a side of square ABCD is:

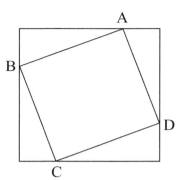

$$\sqrt{(\frac{a}{4})^2 + (\frac{3a}{4})^2} = \sqrt{\frac{5}{8}a^2}$$

The area square ABCD is:

$$(\sqrt{\frac{5a^2}{8}})^2 = \frac{5}{8}a^2 = \frac{5}{8}k$$

Answer $\frac{5}{8}k$ cm²   (4 marks)

16   ABC and DEA are straight lines. BE is parallel to CD. $\angle DAC = 45°$, $\angle ACD = 50°$

Work out the size of $\angle AEB$.

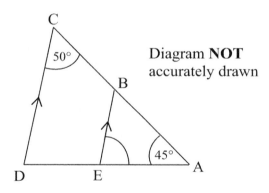

Diagram **NOT** accurately drawn

BE is parallel to $CD \Rightarrow \angle AEB = \angle ADC$

In triangle ADC, $\angle ADC = 180° - \angle DAC - \angle ACD = 180° - 45° - 50° = 85°$

BE is parallel to $CD \Rightarrow \angle AEB = \angle ADC = 85°$

$\therefore\ \angle AEB = 85°$

Answer   85°   (4 marks)

17   ABCDEFGH is a cuboid.

AB = 20 units, BC = 10 units, BF = 12 units

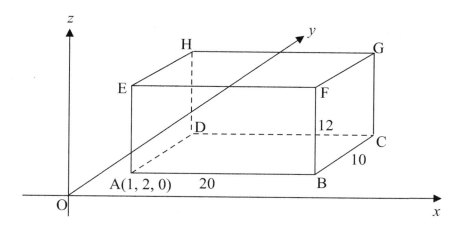

Edges AB, DC, EF and HG are parallel to the *x*-axis. Edges BC, AD, EH and FG are parallel to the *y*-axis. The base ABCD is on the ground.

The coordinates of A are (1, 2, 0).

17(a)   Write down the coordinates of G.

$$G_x = A_x + AB = 1 + 20 = 21$$

$$G_y = A_y + BC = 2 + 10 = 12$$

$$G_z = A_z + AE = 0 + 12 = 12$$

Answer   (21, 12, 12)   (3 marks)

17(b)   Calculate $\left| \overrightarrow{AG} \right|$, the magnitude of $\overrightarrow{AG}$.

Give your answer to 1 decimal place.

$$\left| \overrightarrow{AG} \right| = \sqrt{(G_x - A_x)^2 + (G_y - A_y)^2 + (G_z - A_z)^2} = \sqrt{(21-1)^2 + (12-2)^2 + (12-0)^2} = 25.4$$

Answer   25.4   (3 marks)

18   OAB is a triangle such that $\overrightarrow{OA} = 2\mathbf{a}$ and $\overrightarrow{AB} = \mathbf{b}$. Point D is the midpoint of OA and

ABC is a straight line such that AB:AC = 4:5.

Express $\overrightarrow{DC}$ in terms of **a** and **b**.

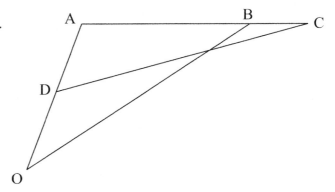

$$AB:AC = 4:5 \Rightarrow \overrightarrow{BC} = \frac{\overrightarrow{AB}}{4} = \frac{\mathbf{b}}{4}$$

$$\text{Point D is the midpoint of } OA \Rightarrow \overrightarrow{DA} = \frac{\overrightarrow{OA}}{2} = \mathbf{a}$$

$$\overrightarrow{DC} = \overrightarrow{DA} + \overrightarrow{AC} = \overrightarrow{DA} + \overrightarrow{AB} + \overrightarrow{BC} = \mathbf{a} + \mathbf{b} + \frac{\mathbf{b}}{4} = \mathbf{a} + \frac{5}{4}\mathbf{b}$$

Answer $\overrightarrow{DC} = \mathbf{a} + \frac{5}{4}\mathbf{b}$ (4 marks)

4

Paper 2 solutions

1   Naomi invests £6000 for 5 years. The investment gets compound interest of 5% per annum.

Work out how much the investment is worth at the end of 5 years.

$6000 \times (1 + 5\%)^5 = 7657.69$

Answer   £7657.69   (2 marks)

2   Here are three numbers written in scientific notation.

Arrange these numbers in ascending order.

3.4×10^{-7} 5.5×10^{-8} 2.1×10^{-6}

Answer 5.5×10^{-8} 3.4×10^{-7} 2.1×10^{-6}

(2 marks)

3   $x : y = 4 : 5$ and $a : b = 5x : 3y$

Work out $a : b$

Give your answer in its simplest form.

$\dfrac{a}{b} = \dfrac{5x}{3y} = \dfrac{5}{3} \times \dfrac{x}{y} = \dfrac{5}{3} \times \dfrac{4}{5} = \dfrac{4}{3}$

Answer $4 : 3$ (2 marks)

4   Solve $\dfrac{x}{3} + \dfrac{x+2}{5} = 3$

$\dfrac{x}{3} + \dfrac{x+2}{5} = 3 \Rightarrow \dfrac{5x + 3x + 6}{15} = 3 \Rightarrow 8x + 6 = 45 \Rightarrow x = \dfrac{39}{8} = 4.875$

Answer   4.875   (2 marks)

5   Solve the equation $\tan x° + 3 = 2$, for $0 \le x < 360$.

$\tan x° + 3 = 2 \Rightarrow \tan x° = -1 \Rightarrow x° = 180° - 45° = 135°$ or $x° = 360° - 45° = 315°$

Answer $135°$, $315°$ (2 marks)

10

47

6   State the maximum and minimum values of $y = 5\cos\frac{1}{2}x°$ and its period.

$$-1 \le \cos\frac{1}{2}x° \le 1 \Rightarrow -5 \le 5\cos\frac{1}{2}x° \le 5, \text{ period: } \frac{360°}{\frac{1}{2}} = 720°$$

Answer   minimum: -5, maximum: 5, period: 720°

(3 marks)

7   Express $\dfrac{6}{\sqrt{18}}$ as a fraction with a rational denominator.

Give your answer in its simplest form.

$$\frac{6}{\sqrt{18}} = \sqrt{\frac{36}{18}} = \sqrt{2}$$

Answer $\sqrt{2}$ (2 marks)

8   Expand and simplify $(\sin x° - \cos x°)^2$.

Show your working.

$$(\sin x° - \cos x°)^2 = \sin^2 x° + \cos^2 x° - 2\sin x° \cos x° = 1 - 2\sin x° \cos x°$$

Answer $1 - 2\sin x° \cos x°$ (2 marks)

9   Simplify $\dfrac{5a}{2a-1} \times \dfrac{10a-5}{4a^3} \div \dfrac{15}{2a^4}$

$$\frac{5a}{2a-1} \times \frac{10a-5}{4a^3} \div \frac{15}{2a^4} = \frac{\overset{1a}{\cancel{5a}}}{\cancel{2a-1}_1} \times \frac{\overset{5}{\cancel{5(2a-1)}}}{\cancel{4a^3}_2} \times \frac{\overset{1a}{\cancel{2a^4}}}{\cancel{15}_3} = \frac{5a^2}{6}$$

Answer $\dfrac{5a^2}{6}$ (2 marks)

10   Factorise fully $3x^3 - 12x$

$$3x^3 - 12x = 3x(x^2 - 4) = 3x(x-2)(x+2)$$

Answer $3x(x-2)(x+2)$ (2 marks)

11   The perimeter of an isosceles triangle flower bed, ABC, is 28 m of rope, with
      AB = AC , and ∠A = 120° .

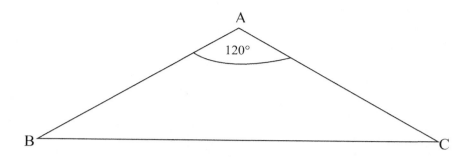

      Work out the length of AB.

      Give your answer to 1 decimal place.

      $AB = AC$, $\angle A = 120° \Rightarrow \angle B = \angle C = \dfrac{180° - 120°}{2} = 30°$

      $AB + AC + BC = 28 \Rightarrow 2AB + BC = 28 \Rightarrow 2AB + AB \times \cos \angle B \times 2 = 28$

      $AB = \dfrac{28}{2 + 2\cos \angle B} = \dfrac{14}{1 + \cos 30°} = 7.5$

               Answer   7.5 m   (4 marks)

12   A sphere and a cone have the same volume. The base of the cone and the sphere have the same radius r cm.

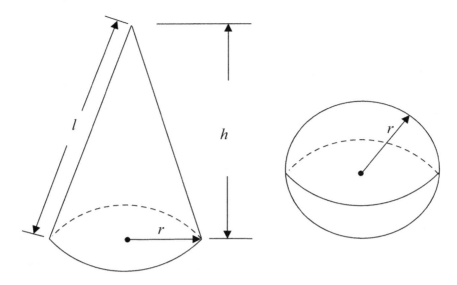

Work out the curved surface area of cone in terms of r.

The sphere and the cone have the same volume,

$$\therefore \ \frac{1}{3}\pi r^2 h = \frac{4}{3}\pi r^3 \Rightarrow h = 4r \qquad \text{where } h \text{ is the height of the cone.}$$

l is the slant height,

$$l = \sqrt{h^2 + r^2} = \sqrt{(4r)^2 + r^2} = \sqrt{17}r$$

$\therefore$ The curved surface area of cone is:

$$\pi r l = \pi r \times \sqrt{17}r = \sqrt{17}\pi r^2$$

Answer $\sqrt{17}\pi r^2$ cm^2 (4 marks)

13   ABC and DEA are straight lines. BE is parallel to CD. $\angle AEB = 85°$, BE = 8 cm, CD = 10 cm, AE = 6 cm.

Work out the length of AC. Give your answer to 2 decimal places.

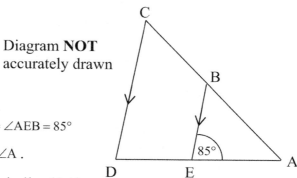

Diagram **NOT** accurately drawn

BE is parallel to CD, $\therefore \angle ADC = \angle AEB = 85°$

Triangles ABE and ACD share $\angle A$.

$\therefore$ Triangles ABE and ACD are similar (AA).

$\dfrac{BE}{CD} = \dfrac{AE}{AD} \Rightarrow AD = AE\dfrac{CD}{BE}$

In triangle ACD, $\quad AC^2 = AD^2 + CD^2 - 2AD \times CD \cos \angle ADC$

$AC = \sqrt{AD^2 + CD^2 - 2AD \times CD \cos \angle ADC}$

$= \sqrt{(AE\dfrac{CD}{BE})^2 + CD^2 - 2AE\dfrac{CD}{BE} \times CD \cos \angle ADC}$

$= \sqrt{(6 \times \dfrac{10}{8})^2 + 10^2 - 2 \times 6 \times \dfrac{10}{8} \times 10 \times \cos 85°} = 11.97$

       Answer   11.97 cm   (4 marks)

4

14   This shape consists of a sector of a circle with 2 identical right-angled triangles.

Take $\pi = 3.14$.

Calculate the area of this shape.

Give your answer to 2 decimal places.

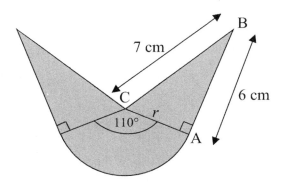

In right-angled triangle ABC, $r = \sqrt{BC^2 - AB^2} = \sqrt{7^2 - 6^2} = \sqrt{13}$

The area of this shape can be calculated as follows.

$$\frac{AC \times AB}{2} \times 2 + \frac{110}{360} \times \pi \times r^2 = \frac{\sqrt{13} \times 6}{2} \times 2 + \frac{110}{360} \times 3.14 \times 13 = 34.11$$

Answer   34.11 cm²   (5 marks)

15   The diagram shows two circles. One has centre A and a radius of 8 cm. The other

has centre B and a radius of 10 cm. AB = 12 cm and the circles intersect at P and Q.

Calculate the length of PQ.

Give your answer to 1 decimal place.

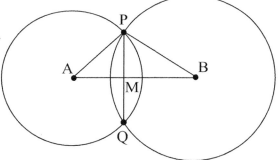

In triangle ABP, $\cos \angle A = \dfrac{AP^2 + AB^2 - PB^2}{2AP \times AB} = \dfrac{8^2 + 12^2 - 10^2}{2 \times 8 \times 12} = \dfrac{9}{16}$

$\sin \angle A = \sqrt{1 - \cos^2 \angle A} = \sqrt{1 - (\dfrac{9}{16})^2} = \dfrac{5}{16}\sqrt{7}$

$PQ = 2PM = 2AP \times \sin \angle A = 2 \times 8 \times \dfrac{5}{16}\sqrt{7} = 5\sqrt{7} = 13.2$

Answer   13.2 cm   (5 marks)

10

16   Here is an L-shape. All lengths are in centimetres.

The shape has area A cm².

Show that $A = w^2 + x^2 - wx$

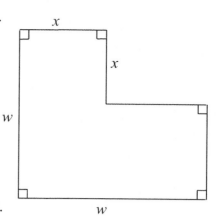

The area of the shape can be calculated as follows.

$A = w^2 - x \times (w - x) = w^2 + x^2 - wx$

$\therefore A = w^2 + x^2 - wx$ (4 marks)

17   The tent shown in the diagram has a base that is 2.5 units wide and 4.0 units long.
The height of the tent is 1.5 units. The ends are isosceles triangles AE = ED, BF =
FC, and perpendicular to the base.

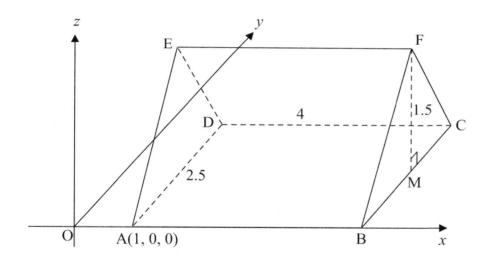

The base ABCD is on the ground. The coordinates of A are $(1, 0, 0)$.

17(a) Find out the coordinates of B.

$B_x = A_x + AB = 1 + 4 = 5$,

$B_y = A_y = 0$

$B_z = A_z = 0$

Answer $(5, 0, 0)$ (3 marks)

17(b)   Find out the coordinates of F.

$F_x = B_x = 5$

$F_y = B_y + BM = 0 + \dfrac{BC}{2} = 1.25$

$F_z = B_z + MF = 0 + 1.5 = 1.5$

Answer   (5, 1.25, 1.5)   (3 marks)

17(c)   Calculate $\left|\overrightarrow{BF}\right|$, the magnitude of $\overrightarrow{BF}$.

Give your answer to 2 decimal places.

M is the midpoint of BC.

$\left|\overrightarrow{BF}\right| = \sqrt{(F_x - B_x)^2 + (F_y - B_y)^2 + (F_z - B_z)^2} = \sqrt{(5-5)^2 + (1.25-0)^2 + (1.5-0)^2} = 1.95$

Answer   1.95   (3 marks)

6

18   OABC is a parallelogram. BCD is a straight line. BD = 3BC. M is the midpoint of OC.

$\overrightarrow{OA} = \mathbf{x}$, $\overrightarrow{AB} = \mathbf{y}$.

Show by a vector method that AM is parallel to OD.

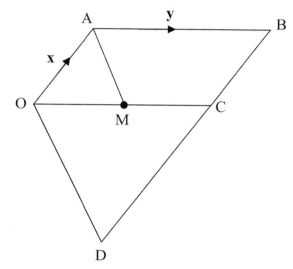

OABC is a parallelogram. BCD is a straight line $\Rightarrow$ CB = OA

$BD = 3BC \Rightarrow \overrightarrow{DB} = 3\mathbf{x}$

M is the midpoint of OC $\Rightarrow \overrightarrow{OM} = \dfrac{\overrightarrow{AB}}{2} = \dfrac{\mathbf{y}}{2}$

$\overrightarrow{OD} = \overrightarrow{OA} + \overrightarrow{AB} - \overrightarrow{DB} = \mathbf{x} + \mathbf{y} - 3\mathbf{x} = \mathbf{y} - 2\mathbf{x}$

$\overrightarrow{AM} = \overrightarrow{OM} - \overrightarrow{OA} = \dfrac{\mathbf{y}}{2} - \mathbf{x} = \dfrac{\overrightarrow{OD}}{2}$

∴ AM is parallel to OD   (4 marks)

Paper 3 solutions

1   Emma buys a jumper.

   20% VAT is added to the price of the jumper. Emma has to pay a total of £60.

   What is the price of the jumper with **no** VAT added?

   $x(1+20\%) = 60 \Rightarrow x = 50$

   Answer   £50   (2 marks)

2   Work out the value of $2.2 \times 10^5 \times (4 \times 10^3)$

   Give your answer in scientific notation.

   $2.2 \times 10^5 \times (4 \times 10^3) = 2.2 \times 4 \times 10^{5+3} = 8.8 \times 10^8$

   Answer 8.8×10^8 (2 marks)

3   Find $|\mathbf{p}|$, the magnitude of vector $\mathbf{p} = \begin{pmatrix} 10 \\ 8 \\ -40 \end{pmatrix}$.

   $|\mathbf{p}| = \sqrt{10^2 + 8^2 + (-40)^2} = 42$

   Answer   42   (2 marks)

4   Solve the simultaneous equations

   $2x - 4y = 10$

   $2x + y = 30$

   $2x - 4y = 10$ (1)

   $2x + y = 30$ (2)

   Eq. (2) - Eq. (1) $\Rightarrow 5y = 20 \Rightarrow y = 4$, $x = \dfrac{30 - y}{2} = 13$ from Eq. (2).

   Answer $x = 13$, $y = 4$ (2 marks)

5   Solve the equation $4 \sin x° + 3 = 2$, for $0 \le x < 360$.

   Give your answers to 1 decimal place.

   $4 \sin x° + 3 = 2 \Rightarrow \sin x° = -\dfrac{1}{4} \Rightarrow x° = 360° - 14.5° = 345.5°$ or $x° = 180° + 14.5° = 194.5°$

   Answer   194.5°, 345.5°   (2 marks)

10

6   State the maximum and minimum values of $y = 5\sin 2x° - 2$ and its period.

$-1 \le \sin 2x° \le 1 \Rightarrow -5 \le 5\sin 2x° \le 5 \Rightarrow -7 \le 5\sin 2x° - 2 \le 3$, period: $\dfrac{360°}{2} = 180°$

Answer   minimum: -7, maximum: 3, period: $180°$

(3 marks)

7   Express $\dfrac{\sqrt{30}}{\sqrt{2}}$ as a fraction with a rational denominator.

Give your answer in its simplest form.

$\dfrac{\sqrt{30}}{\sqrt{2}} = \sqrt{\dfrac{30}{2}} = \sqrt{15}$

Answer $\sqrt{15}$

(2 marks)

8   Expand and simplify $(\sqrt{x} + \dfrac{1}{\sqrt{x}})^2$, where $x > 0$.

Show your working.

$(\sqrt{x} + \dfrac{1}{\sqrt{x}})^2 = x + \dfrac{1}{x} + 2 \times \sqrt{x} \times \dfrac{1}{\sqrt{x}} = x + \dfrac{1}{x} + 2$

Answer $x + \dfrac{1}{x} + 2$

(2 marks)

9   Simplify $\dfrac{x^2 - 2x + 1}{x^2 - 6x + 5}$, $x \ne 1$, $x \ne 5$

$\dfrac{x^2 - 2x + 1}{x^2 - 6x + 5} = \dfrac{(x-1)^2}{(x-1)(x-5)} = \dfrac{x-1}{x-5}$

Answer $\dfrac{x-1}{x-5}$

(2 marks)

10   Factorise fully $4c^3 d - 9cd^3$

$4c^3 d - 9cd^3 = cd(4c^2 - 9d^2) = cd(2c - 3d)(2c + 3d)$

Answer $cd(2c - 3d)(2c + 3d)$

(2 marks)

11

11   Here is a triangle.

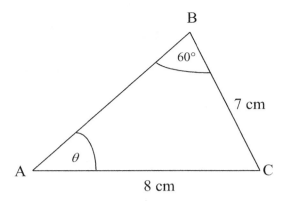

Work out the angle θ.

Give your answer to 1 decimal place.

$$\frac{8}{\sin 60°} = \frac{7}{\sin \theta} \Rightarrow \sin \theta = \frac{7}{8}\sin 60° \Rightarrow \theta = 49.3°$$

Answer   49.3°   (5 marks)

12   The diagram shows a solid prism. The top EFGH is a rectangle of width 20 cm and length 30 cm, the base ABCD is rectangle of width 20 cm and length 50 cm. The line joining the centres of the top and the base is perpendicular to both and is 40 cm long.

Work out the volume of the prism.

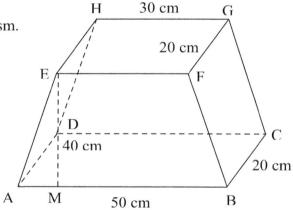

Draw a line EM which is perpendicular AB. EM = 40 cm.

The prism has a height of 20 cm and the cross section with a trapezium.

The volume of the prism is:

$$\frac{EF + AB}{2} \times EM \times BC = \frac{30 + 50}{2} \times 40 \times 20 = 32000$$

Answer   32000 cm³   (5 marks)

13   The diagram shows triangle ABC. AB = AC.

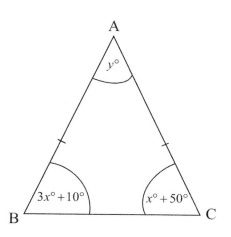

Find the value of $y°$.

Show your working clearly.

$AB = AC \Rightarrow \angle B = \angle C \Rightarrow 3x° + 10° = x° + 50° \Rightarrow x° = 20°$

$\angle A + \angle B + \angle C = 180° \Rightarrow \angle A = 180° - 2\angle C = 180° - 2(20° + 50°) = 40°$

$\therefore y° = 40°$

Answer   40°   (5 marks)

14   The shape consists of two overlapping circles below.

Find the perimeter of this shape.

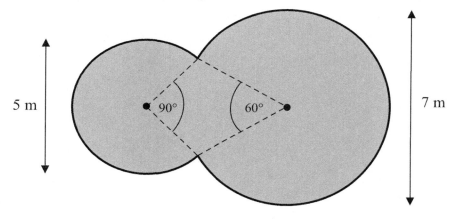

Take $\pi = 3.14$.

Give your answer to 2 decimal places.

$(1 - \dfrac{90}{360}) \times \pi \times 5 + (1 - \dfrac{60}{360}) \times \pi \times 7 = 30.09$

Answer   30.09 m   (5 marks)

15   A hot air balloon is hovering above the ground. Emma and Jack are looking up at

the hot air balloon. In the diagram below, E, J and B represent the positions of

Emma, Jack and the balloon respectively.

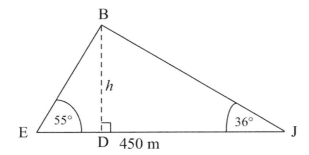

The angle of elevation of the balloon from Emma is $55°$

The angle of elevation of the balloon from Jack is $36°$

Emma and Jack are 450 metres apart on level ground.

Calculate the height of the hot air balloon above the ground.

Give your answer to 1 decimal place.

From B, draw line BD which is perpendicular to EJ.

In right-angled triangle BDE, $ED = \dfrac{h}{\tan \angle E} = \dfrac{h}{\tan 55°}$

In right-angled triangle BDJ, $DJ = \dfrac{h}{\tan \angle J} = \dfrac{h}{\tan 36°}$

$ED + DJ = 450 \Rightarrow \dfrac{h}{\tan 55°} + \dfrac{h}{\tan 36°} = 450 \Rightarrow h = \dfrac{450 \times \tan 55° \times \tan 36°}{\tan 36° + \tan 55°} = 216.7$

      Answer   216.7 m   (5 marks)

16   A company produces mugs in two sizes.

Small mugs are 6 cm high and can hold 100 cm³ of liquid.

Large mugs are 12 cm high and are identical in shape to small mugs.

Work out the volume of a large mug.

$\dfrac{\text{volume of large mug}}{\text{volume of small mug}} = (\dfrac{\text{height of large mug}}{\text{height of small mug}})^3$

$\text{volume of large mug} = (\dfrac{\text{height of large mug}}{\text{height of small mug}})^3 \times \text{volume of small mug} = (\dfrac{12}{6})^3 \times 100 = 800$

      Answer   800 cm³   (4 marks)

9

17   ABCD is a pyramid. ABC is an isosceles triangle with AB = AC = 10 units and BC = 12 units. BCD is an isosceles triangle with BD = CD = 26 units. D is vertically above A and $\angle BAD = \angle CAD = 90°$.

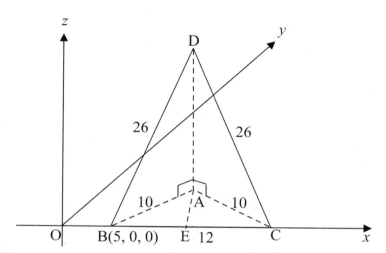

The base ABC is on the ground. The coordinates of B are (5, 0, 0).

Find out the coordinates of D.

E is the midpoint of BC.

In right-angled ACD, $AD = \sqrt{CD^2 - AC^2} = \sqrt{26^2 - 10^2} = 24$

In right-angled ACE, $EA = \sqrt{AC^2 - EC^2} = \sqrt{AC^2 - (\frac{BC}{2})^2} = \sqrt{10^2 - 6^2} = 8$

$D_x = B_x + BE = 5 + 6 = 11$

$D_y = EA = 8$

$D_z = AD = 24$

    Answer   (11, 8, 24)   (5 marks)

18   PQR is a triangle. W is the midpoint of PQ. X is the point on QR such that

QX : XR = 3 : 1. PRY is a straight line. $\overrightarrow{PQ} = \mathbf{a}$, $\overrightarrow{PR} = \mathbf{b}$, PR : RY = 2 : 1.

Use a vector method to show that WXY is a straight line.

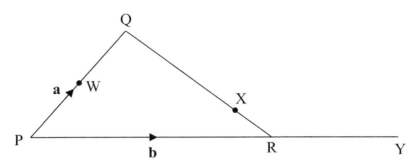

$\overrightarrow{QR} = \mathbf{b} - \mathbf{a}$

$$QX : XR = 3 : 1 \Rightarrow \overrightarrow{QX} = \frac{3}{4}\overrightarrow{QR} = \frac{3}{4}(\mathbf{b} - \mathbf{a}), \ \overrightarrow{XR} = \frac{\overrightarrow{QR}}{4} = \frac{\mathbf{b} - \mathbf{a}}{4}$$

$$PR : RY = 2 : 1 \Rightarrow \overrightarrow{RY} = \frac{\overrightarrow{PR}}{2} = \frac{\mathbf{b}}{2}$$

$$\overrightarrow{WX} = \overrightarrow{WQ} + \overrightarrow{QX} = \frac{\mathbf{a}}{2} + \frac{3}{4}(\mathbf{b} - \mathbf{a}) = \frac{3\mathbf{b} - \mathbf{a}}{4}$$

$$\overrightarrow{XY} = \overrightarrow{XR} + \overrightarrow{RY} = \frac{\mathbf{b} - \mathbf{a}}{4} + \frac{\mathbf{b}}{2} = \frac{3\mathbf{b} - \mathbf{a}}{4}$$

$\therefore \overrightarrow{WX} = \overrightarrow{XY}$

$\overrightarrow{WX}$ and $\overrightarrow{XY}$ share the same point X.

$\therefore$ WXY is a straight line.

(5 marks)

Paper 4 solutions

1   An antiques dealer buys a vase for £400. He sells the vase for 50% more than the

price he paid for it.

For how much does the dealer sell the vase?

$400 \times (1 + 50\%) = 600$

Answer   £600   (2 marks)

2   A sunflower seed weighs 3.5×10^{-5} kilograms, the weight of a sesame seed is 9% of

the weight of a sunflower seed.

Calculate the weight of a sesame seed in kilograms.

Give your answer in scientific notation.

$3.5 \times 10^{-5} \times 9\% = 3.15 \times 10^{-6}$

Answer 3.15×10^{-6} kilograms   (2 marks)

3   Calculate the distance from A(10, 15, 32) to B(6, 9, 20).

$d = \sqrt{(A_x - B_x)^2 + (A_y - B_y)^2 + (A_z - B_z)^2} = \sqrt{(10-6)^2 + (15-9)^2 + (32-20)^2} = 14$

Answer   14 units   (2 marks)

4   Emma is solving $3x^2 + 9x = 0$

She uses the following method:

$3x^2 + 9x = 0 \xrightarrow{\text{subtract } 9x \text{ from both sides}} 3x^2 = -9x \xrightarrow{\text{divide both sides by } 3x} x = -3$

Evaluate her method and her answer.

Cannot divide by $3x$ as it could be zero and the solution $x = 0$ could be missed.

It should have solved as follows.

$3x^2 + 9x = 0 \Rightarrow 3x(x+3) = 0 \Rightarrow x = 0$ **or** $x = -3$ (2 marks)

5   Solve $25\sin^2 x° = 1$ for $0 \le x < 360$.

Give your answers to 1 decimal place.

$25\sin^2 x° = 1 \Rightarrow \sin x° = \pm 0.2 \Rightarrow$

$x° = \sin^{-1} 0.2 \Rightarrow x° = 11.5°$ or $180° - 11.5° = 168.5°$

$x° = \sin^{-1}(-0.2) \Rightarrow x° = 180° + 11.5° = 191.5°$ or $360° - 11.5° = 348.5°$

Answer $11.5°, 168.5°, 191.5°, 348.5°$ (4 marks)

12

6 State the maximum and minimum values of $y = 5\sin(x-50)° + 3$ and its period.

$-1 \le \sin(x-50)° \le 1 \Rightarrow -5 \le 5\sin(x-50)° \le 5 \Rightarrow -2 \le 5\sin(x-50)° + 3 \le 8$,

period: $360°$

Answer   minimum: -2, maximum: 8, period: $360°$

(3 marks)

7 Express $\sqrt{2} + \dfrac{8}{\sqrt{2}}$ as a fraction with a rational denominator.

Give your answer in its simplest form.

$\sqrt{2} + \dfrac{8}{\sqrt{2}} = \sqrt{2} + \dfrac{8\sqrt{2}}{2} = 5\sqrt{2}$

Answer $5\sqrt{2}$

(2 marks)

8 Write as a single fraction $\dfrac{10}{x^2 - 25} - \dfrac{1}{x-5}$, $x \ne 5$, $x \ne -5$

Give your answer in its simplest form.

$\dfrac{10}{x^2 - 25} - \dfrac{1}{x-5} = \dfrac{10}{(x-5)(x+5)} - \dfrac{x+5}{(x-5)(x+5)} = \dfrac{10-x-5}{(x-5)(x+5)} = -\dfrac{1}{x+5}$

Answer $-\dfrac{1}{x+5}$

(2 marks)

9 Simplify $(2x^3 y^2)^4$

$(2x^3 y^2)^4 = 2^4 x^{3\times4} y^{2\times4} = 16x^{12} y^8$

Answer $16x^{12} y^8$

(2 marks)

10 Factorise fully $(x+5)^3 - (x+5)^2 (x-5)$.

$(x+5)^3 - (x+5)^2 (x-5) = (x+5)^2 (x+5-x+5) = 10(x+5)^2$

Answer $10(x+5)^2$

(2 marks)

11

11   Triangle ABC has perimeter 16cm

AB = 5 cm.

BC = 4 cm.

Calculate the size of the biggest angle in triangle ABC.

Give your answer to 1 decimal place.

$AC = 16 - 5 - 4 = 7$ which is the longest side in the triangle. Sketch triangle ABC

below.

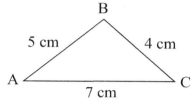

∴ ∠B is the biggest angle in the triangle.

$$\cos \angle B = \frac{AB^2 + BC^2 - AC^2}{2 \times AB \times BC} = \frac{25 + 16 - 49}{2 \times 5 \times 4} = -\frac{1}{5} \Rightarrow \angle B = 101.5°$$

Answer   101.5°   (3 marks)

12   Solid **A** and Solid **B** are mathematically similar.

Solid **A** has a volume of 50 cm³

Solid **A** has surface area 30 cm²

Solid **B** has surface area 270 cm²

Calculate the volume of solid **B**.

The volume of solid **B** can be calculated as follows:

$$\sqrt[3]{\frac{\text{Volume } \mathbf{B}}{\text{Volume } \mathbf{A}}} = \sqrt{\frac{\text{Area } \mathbf{B}}{\text{Area } \mathbf{A}}} \Rightarrow \text{Volume } \mathbf{B} = \left(\sqrt{\frac{\text{Area } \mathbf{B}}{\text{Area } \mathbf{A}}}\right)^3 \times \text{Volume } \mathbf{A} = (\sqrt{\frac{270}{30}})^3 \times 50 = 1350$$

Answer   1350 cm³   (3 marks)

6

13   PQRS is an isosceles trapezium. Each side of the trapezium is a tangent to the circle.

The radius of the circle is r cm.

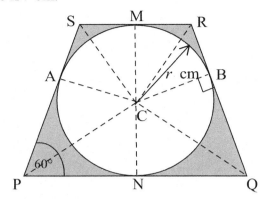

13(a) Work out the perimeter of the isosceles trapezium.

Give your answer in terms of r.

The perimeter of the isosceles trapezium $= 4\text{PN} + 4\text{SM}$ (1)

$$\text{PN} = \frac{\text{CN}}{\tan \angle \text{CPN}} = \frac{r}{\tan 30°} = \sqrt{3}\,r \qquad\qquad (2)$$

$$\text{SM} = \text{CM} \times \tan \angle \text{SCM} = r\tan 30° = \frac{\sqrt{3}}{3}\,r \qquad (3)$$

The perimeter of the isosceles trapezium is:

$$4\sqrt{3}r + 4 \times \frac{\sqrt{3}}{3}\,r = \frac{16\sqrt{3}}{3}\,r$$

Answer $\dfrac{16\sqrt{3}}{3}\,r$ cm   (3 marks)

13(b) Work out the area of the shaded region.

Give your answer in terms of r.

The area of the isosceles trapezium is:

$$\frac{\text{SR} + \text{PQ}}{2} \times \text{MN} = \frac{2\text{SM} + 2\text{PN}}{2} \times 2r = (\text{SM} + \text{PN}) \times 2r = \frac{4\sqrt{3}}{3}\,r \times 2r = \frac{8\sqrt{3}}{3}\,r^2$$

The area of the shaded region is $\dfrac{8\sqrt{3}}{3}\,r^2 - \pi r^2$

Answer $\left(\dfrac{8\sqrt{3}}{3}\,r^2 - \pi r^2\right)$ cm^2 (3 marks)

6

14   The base for a rocking horse is made from the arc of a circular piece of wood, with a triangular section ABO cut off. The radius of the circle is 90 cm and $\angle AOB = 62°$.

Take $\pi = 3.14$.

Give your answer to 2 decimal places.

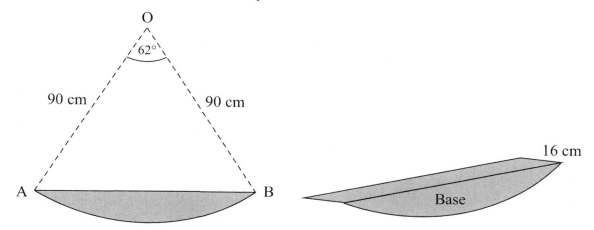

14(a)   Calculate the area of the segment.

$$\frac{62}{360} \times \pi \times OA^2 - \frac{OA \times OB \times \sin 62°}{2} = \frac{62}{360} \times 3.14 \times 90^2 - \frac{90 \times 90 \times \sin 62°}{2} = 804.36$$

Answer   804.36 cm²   (3 marks)

14(b)   Calculate the volume of wood used to make the base (16 cm wide) of the rocking horse.

$804.36 \times 16 = 12869.76$

Answer   12869.76 cm³   (3 marks)

6

15   Three lighthouses, A, B and C are situated on the seaside.

Lighthouse A is 30 km due south of lighthouse B.

Lighthouse B is 50 km from lighthouse C.

Lighthouse C is on a bearing of 120° from lighthouse A.

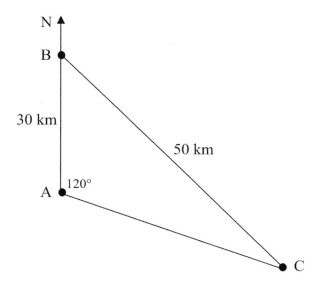

Calculate the bearing of lighthouse C from lighthouse B.

In triangle ABC, $\dfrac{AB}{\sin \angle C} = \dfrac{BC}{\sin \angle A} \Rightarrow \sin \angle C = \dfrac{AB \sin \angle A}{BC} = \dfrac{30 \sin 120°}{50} \Rightarrow \angle C = 31°$

$\angle NBC = \angle A + \angle C = 120° + 31° = 151°$

   Answer   151°   (3 marks)

16    $A(1\frac{1}{2},\ \frac{1}{4})$, $B(2\frac{1}{2},\ 2\frac{1}{4})$ and $C(3,\ 3\frac{1}{4})$ are points on a coordinate grid. Show that

the three points are on a straight line.

The gradient of AB: $K_1 = \dfrac{2\frac{1}{4} - \frac{1}{4}}{2\frac{1}{2} - 1\frac{1}{2}} = 2$

The gradient of BC: $K_2 = \dfrac{3\frac{1}{4} - 2\frac{1}{4}}{3 - 2\frac{1}{2}} = 2$

$K_1 = K_2$

∴ The three points are on a straight line.

                                   (4 marks)

7

17   ABCDEFGH is a basket. The top ABCD is a square of side 35 units and the base
      EFGH is square of side 25 units. The line joining the centres of the top and the base
      is perpendicular to both and is 40 units long.

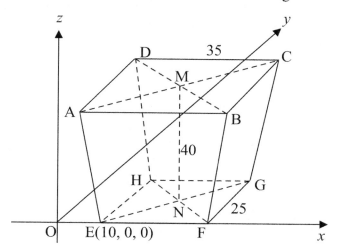

The base EFGH is on the ground. The coordinates of E are (10, 0, 0).

17(a)   Find out the coordinates of C.

$$C_x = E_x + \frac{EF}{2} + \frac{AB}{2} = 10 + \frac{25}{2} + \frac{35}{2} = 40$$

$$C_y = E_y + \frac{FG}{2} + \frac{BC}{2} = 0 + \frac{25}{2} + \frac{35}{2} = 30$$

$$C_z = E_z + NM = 0 + 40 = 40$$

          Answer   (40, 30, 40)   (3 marks)

17(b)   Calculate $\left|\overrightarrow{EC}\right|$, the magnitude of $\overrightarrow{EC}$.

        Give your answer to 1 decimal place.

$$\left|\overrightarrow{EC}\right| = \sqrt{(C_x - E_x)^2 + (C_y - E_y)^2 + (C_z - E_z)^2} = \sqrt{(40-10)^2 + (30-0)^2 + (40-0)^2} = 58.3$$

          Answer   58.3   (3 marks)

6

18   ABCDEFGH is a cuboid.

K lies one quarter of the way along HG.

L lies one third of the way along FG.

$\overrightarrow{AD} = \mathbf{u}$, $\overrightarrow{AB} = \mathbf{v}$, $\overrightarrow{AE} = \mathbf{w}$

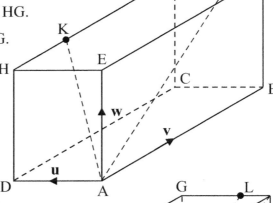

18(a)   Find the vector $\overrightarrow{AK}$, in terms of $\mathbf{u}$, $\mathbf{v}$ and $\mathbf{w}$.

$$\overrightarrow{AK} = \overrightarrow{AE} + \overrightarrow{EK} = \overrightarrow{AE} + \overrightarrow{EH} + \overrightarrow{HK} = \mathbf{w} + \mathbf{u} + \frac{\mathbf{v}}{4}$$

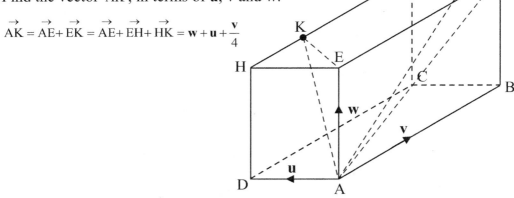

Answer $\overrightarrow{AK} = \mathbf{w} + \mathbf{u} + \dfrac{\mathbf{v}}{4}$ (3 marks)

18(b)   Find the vector $\overrightarrow{AL}$, in terms of $\mathbf{u}$, $\mathbf{v}$ and $\mathbf{w}$.

$$\overrightarrow{AL} = \overrightarrow{AF} + \overrightarrow{FL} = \overrightarrow{AB} + \overrightarrow{BF} + \overrightarrow{FL} = \mathbf{v} + \mathbf{w} + \frac{\mathbf{u}}{3}$$

Answer $\overrightarrow{AL} = \mathbf{v} + \mathbf{w} + \dfrac{\mathbf{u}}{3}$ (3 marks)

6

Printed in Great Britain
by Amazon